CW01500242

Britain, Tough on Crime?

on Crime?

A View of the British Criminal Justice System
Through the Newspaper Headlines

DAVID FRASER

THE CHOIR PRESS

First published in the United Kingdom in 2024 by
The Choir Press

ISBN 978-1-78963-455-6

About the Author

David Fraser was educated at the London School of Economics and Political Science and later at the University of Bristol where he obtained his M. Phil higher degree. He worked in industry and as a teacher in a junior school. He served for many years as a senior probation officer in what is now the National Probation Service, in busy Inner London magistrates' courts and in prisons in the capital and the south-west. He also worked as a Criminal Intelligence Analyst with the National Criminal Intelligence Service (now the National Crime Agency) for many years.

His first book, *A Land Fit for Criminals*, was recommended for the George Orwell Prize in Literature. He has lectured widely on the subject of crime and sentencing, in Britain and abroad, and has given evidence to a number of government inquiries in England and Wales into crime, sentencing and prisons.

He has campaigned for many years, via the press, radio and television, for our sentencing laws to be changed to ensure they protect the public from crime.

His books and many articles are based on 40 years of criminal justice research.

He is married and lives with his wife in the West Country. He has two adult children and two grandchildren.

Books by David Fraser

Non-Fiction:

A Land Fit for Criminals, An Insider's View of Crime, Punishment and Justice (pub. The Choir Press, 2022; first published by The Book Guild Ltd, 2006).

Licence to Kill, Britain's Surrender to Violence (pub. The Choir Press, 2022; first published by The Book Guild Ltd, 2018).

Badlands NZ: A Land Fit for Criminals (pub. Howling at the Moon Publishing Ltd, New Zealand, 2011).

Acknowledgements

I am indebted to Theodore Dalrymple for
his help and support with this project

In Memory of Roger Dean

Prologue

For three reasons, no intellectual ever increased his prestige by suggesting that the penalties for crime were too lenient. First, legal punishments in the past have often been brutal, cruel or horribly severe; second, because such a suggestion is likely to be considered a manifestation of sadism; and third, because to see things from the point of view of the criminal, rather than from that of the victim or of society as a whole, is now regarded not only as broad- and generous-minded but as being uncommon. And what is the point of an intellectual if he doesn't think differently from most people?

But if punishment can be too severe, it follows that it can also be too lenient (unless the whole idea of punishment is rejected altogether). In the following pages, my friend David Fraser has collected from newspaper headlines instances of convicted violent criminals who have been left by the British criminal justice system – one might almost say, challenged by it – to offend again, and often again and again.

It is true, of course, that the evidence here presented is anecdotal; but at some point, an anecdote that can be repeated hundreds of times ceases to be a mere anecdote. In fact, the statistics establish that the cases here included are *not* atypical, but rather point to a systematic failing. Some of the stories are so absurd or ludicrous that they would be funny were it not for their terrible consequences.

A compiler of a book such as this is between the Scylla of being accused of anecdotalism if he includes too few cases and the Charybdis of being repetitious if he includes too many. I think this short book is a happy compromise.

The reader should constantly bear in mind that the rate of reoffending and of reconviction are not the same and would only be the same if the perpetrator of every crime were convicted. This is far from being the case. The evidence from many sources suggests that, in Britain, fewer than one in twenty crimes leads to a conviction. Since the perpetration of crimes is not evenly distributed through the population, most people who are convicted of something have committed more, and often many more, crimes than those with which they have ever been charged.

Readers should also beware of those who tell them that Britain has a high rate of imprisonment per 100,000 of population by comparison with other Western European countries. That this is a bogus statistic is easily demonstrated by the fact that if no crime had ever been committed in Britain, it would be an outrageous injustice if there were only one prisoner, though this would mean a very low rate indeed of imprisonment per 100,000 of the population. The relevant comparative statistic is not the number of prisoners per 100,000 of the population but the number of crimes per prisoner.

It would be good also if readers could bear in mind as well that while it is true that most criminals have relatively unfortunate backgrounds, so too do their victims.

Theodore Dalrymple

The Achievements of Sixty Years of British Criminal Sentencing Policy

Crime has been made:

Easier

Safer

More Rewarding

The following examples have mostly been taken from items
that have appeared in the British press over the last
27 years.

Unless otherwise stated, crime statistics have been taken from
government criminal statistics for England and Wales for the
relevant years.
These are summarised in two books, both originally published by
The Book Guild and now available from The Choir Press:
Licence to Kill, Britain's Surrender to Violence, David Fraser (2018)
and
*A Land Fit For Criminals, An Insider's View of Crime, Punishment
and Justice in the UK,* David Fraser (2006).

One in nine murderers is freed from prison after serving fewer than ten years

MailOnline, 3rd January 2012, 'Time Served for Murder'.

Between 1900 and the present, hundreds of killers have been released from sentences of life imprisonment to kill again

Second homicide convictions per five million of the population have increased four-fold since 1964

Compiled from Home Office Bulletins and 'Homicide Firearm Offences and Intimate Violence; Crime in England and Wales Supplementary Volumes', for the years 1900–2011, as well as newspaper reports for the same period.

Office for National Statistics, Crime Statistics, Focus on Violent Crime and Sex Offences, 2013/14

'The real me is a loving person.' How Karolina killer Clive Hayes made his case for release after three child rapes

Bristol Evening Post, 12th August 2006

Clive Hayes was given three years' imprisonment for raping two schoolgirls, aged 14 and 15, in 1973.

1975: Within weeks of his release, Hayes dragged another 15-year-old girl from the street into his car. He took her to his bedsit where he tied her up and raped her at knifepoint.

He was given a 'life sentence' of imprisonment.

1995: The Parole Board released him, saying 'He is an acceptable risk.'

2006: Hayes abducted a 20-year-old Polish care worker, Karolina Mikolajewska, and murdered her in his bedsit near Bristol. Shortly afterwards, he was killed in a car crash.

Note: *Is it not possible that the 'punishment' of just two years in prison (due to remission) for abducting and raping two schoolgirls acted as a 'green light' for Hayes? Would he have abducted another schoolgirl within weeks of his release if he had been made to serve 30 years in the first place? Would Karolina Mikolajewska not still be alive if his life sentence had meant what it said and kept him in prison for the rest of his life?*

A murder a week by thugs on probation

The Daily Express, 2nd July 1997

I can still see in my dreams but when I wake, the truth hits

The Independent, 14th April 2012

Thirty-three-year-old Shane Jenkin carried out a premeditated, sustained, vicious attack on his partner, mother of two, 32-year-old Tina Nash.

He broke her nose and her jaw, throttled her until she was unconscious and then deliberately gouged out both of her eyes with his thumbs. Originally charged with attempted murder, he pleaded guilty to grievous bodily harm.

Jenkin, when he met Tina Nash, had recently been released from prison having served a sentence for grievous bodily harm, inflicting permanent brain damage on a man. He was sentenced at Truro Crown Court to an indefinite period of imprisonment, to serve a minimum of six years, before he could be considered for release.

Note: *Was it reasonable even to contemplate a release after six years following such an abominable crime?*

Two men receive life imprisonment for brutal murder, with minimum tariffs of 11 years and 13 years respectively

http://warband.wordpress.com/category/assault/page/3/

In 2012, Sade Samanter, 21 years, and Ibrahim Dualeh, 34 years, carried out an unprovoked attack on 31-year-old Abdullahi Osman, who died as a result of the injuries he sustained.

His assailants were convicted of murder.

Sade Samanter was sentenced to life imprisonment, with a minimum tariff of 11 years.

Ibrahim Dualeh was sentenced to life imprisonment, with a minimum tariff of 13 years.

Note: *Samanter will be only 32 and Dualeh 43 if released after serving their minimum tariffs.*

Carey attacks prison 'revenge'

The Daily Telegraph, 10th May 1996

In 1996, the Archbishop of Canterbury, Dr George Carey, said:

'Penal policy is weighted too heavily in favour of imprisonment.'

Note: *Government figures showed that in 1954 the prison population for England and Wales was 51.6 prisoners per 1,000 crimes.*

In 1996, when Dr Carey made this statement, it had fallen to 11.0 prisoners per 1,000 crimes.

A 'slap on the wrist' for rape

The Sunday Telegraph, 6th January 2013

'Hundreds of violent criminals, including rapists, are walking free from court after lenient sentences', such as community orders and other non-prison sentences.

The maximum punishment for grievous bodily harm is life imprisonment. It is therefore viewed as one of the most serious forms of violence next to murder and attempted murder

Darwen attacker gets suspended sentence

The Lancashire Telegraph, 1st April 2011

Thirty-six-year-old Barry John Lettherd punched, kicked and kneed his partner, twisted her ankle, spat on her and pulled her hair during the assault. He held a knife to his victim's face and also assaulted a police officer.

He pleaded guilty to two charges of assault and was sentenced to 18 weeks in prison, suspended for two years.

Lettherd was subject to a prison early release licence at the time of the attack and was recalled for 28 days.

Three men unleash vicious attack over wheelie bin dispute

Staffordshire Newsletter, 20th January 2012

In January 2012, three men, Oliver O'Neill (23 years), Daniel Chrapkowski (24 years) and Thomas Lane (24 years) attacked Joseph O'Reilly (23 years) when he asked them why they were tipping over wheelie bins in Manchester City Centre.

All three were convicted of grievous bodily harm.

Joseph O'Reilly was punched to the ground. He was then punched and kicked in the face as he lay defenceless on the pavement. He suffered a broken jaw and bleeding to the brain.

Chrapkowski was given a 12-month suspended prison term.

Lane was given a community order for 12 months.

O'Neill was on bail for another attack when he assaulted O'Reilly. After admitting two other grievous bodily harm (GBH) charges, he was jailed for 27 months.

Note: *Twenty-seven months for three convictions of GBH is the total time* **given**. *Because of remission, total time* **served** *will be between 13 months and 18 months. This represents just over five months' imprisonment for each crime of grievous bodily harm, regarded as the most serious form of violence next to murder and attempted murder.*

Life for addict who stamped man, 83, to death

http://ukcommentators.blogspot.com/2007/09/tonights-early-release-murderers.httml

In 1998, career criminal James Stace was sentenced at Newcastle Upon Tyne Crown Court for 12 offences of robbery and burglary.

His victims, against whom he often used extreme violence, were the elderly and frail. He asked for another 140 offences to be taken into consideration.

He was sentenced to eight years in prison. He was released after serving four years.

Note: *For the total of 152 offences, he was sentenced to eight years' imprisonment. This represents 19 weeks' prison time **given** for each crime. Due to remission, total time **served** was four years or 9.5 weeks for each crime.*

Life for addict who stamped man, 83, to death (continued)

MailOnline, 19th September 2007

http://ukcommentators.blogspot.com/2007/09/tonights-early-release-murderers.httml

In January 2003, James Stace was sentenced to 18 months for robbery and released after serving nine months.

In June 2005, he was sentenced to three years for attempted burglary, and in July 2005, he received 18 months for burglary, to run concurrently.

Already free in October 2006, he was charged with criminal damage at Thames Magistrates' Court.

He was released and three months later, on 29th December 2006, he murdered elderly widower Ferozur Rahman.

Stace (aged 37 years) was sentenced to life imprisonment with a minimum tariff of 28 years.

Note: *He will be eligible for parole in 2034. He will then be 51 years old, and still potentially dangerous.*

'Reoffending rate by killers and rapists is higher than we think,' says Parole Board

MailOnline, 7th January 2011

'I want to give out harsher sentences
but my hands are tied,' says judge

The Daily Express, 3rd September 2009

Cruel stepfather jailed

The Daily Telegraph, 19th July 2014

A ten-year-old girl from Rochdale was deliberately starved by her stepfather. She was fed raw potato peelings.

He was sentenced to three years in jail. The child's mother was given a 15-month suspended sentence.

Note: *The 50% remission rule automatically reduces the three-year sentence to 18 months.*

Angry attacker is given another chance by judge

Derby Evening Telegraph, 6th September 2010

In September 2010, 23-year-old Nathan Stevenson, from Derby, attacked Damien Dilley, aged 38, and knocked him to the ground.

He repeatedly punched him while he was down. The victim suffered a suspected fracture of his eye socket and bleeding to his brain.

Stevenson had previous convictions for violence.

The judge sentenced him to a nine-month jail term, suspended for two years.

Why Was Screwdriver Killer on the Streets?

The Daily Mail, 18th December 2019

Ewan Ireland accumulated 32 previous convictions, many for violence, between the ages of 14 and 18 years.

In 2019, he was 'released under investigation', related to an allegation of robbery at knifepoint.

Later that year, on 14th August, in the centre of Newcastle, he killed 52-year-old Peter Duncan, by stabbing him with a 12" flathead screwdriver he had stolen a few moments before.

This happened moments after they had brushed past each other at the entrance to a shopping centre.

On 17th December 2019, he was convicted of Peter Duncan's murder and sentenced to life imprisonment with a minimum tariff of 15 years.

He became the first criminal to be convicted of murder after being 'released under investigation'.

Note: *He will be eligible for release in 2034, and by virtue of his age at that point, 33 years, and his record, he will still be potentially dangerous.*

Released Under Investigation

Since the Policing and Crime Act 2017, the majority of people arrested, and interviewed under caution, are released under investigation (RUI).

This is the case even for offences of violence.

This means they are released without charge.

They have no restrictions placed upon them.

They have no obligation to report to anyone or return on bail for the offence.

The suspects are told the investigation will remain ongoing and that they will be notified of the outcome in due course.

Note: *Criminals must find it difficult to believe their luck.*

Criminals on probation 'get just one call every six weeks'

The Daily Mail, 14th December 2017

David Braddon breached his probation order eight times before murdering teenager Conner Marshall in Porthcawl, in 2015. He beat him with an iron bar and stamped on him.

At the time of the killing, Braddon was wearing an electronic tag. His movements were being monitored by a private probation company called Working Links.

Working Links said: 'Public protection is our top priority.'

They added: 'All decisions were made and supervised by fully qualified probation workers.'

1,000 women are spared jail after attacking police

The Daily Mail, 11th December 2019

The number of women convicted of attacking a police officer but walking free from court with a fine has doubled in ten years.

Don't Scrimp Justice

The Daily Telegraph, 18th January 2020

At least ten police forces in England and Wales have adopted 'deferred prosecution' schemes whereby offenders are offered four-month rehabilitation in exchange for charges being dropped.

Note: *These schemes ignore the evidence, collected over 60 years by the government, that criminals cannot be 'rehabilitated'. Criminals continue to commit crimes during and after their period of supervision and attendance on reform programmes.*

Waffle behind the failure to deal with knife crime scourge

The Daily Mail, 7th March 2019

Confronted with the surge in knife crime, Sajid Javid said that 'serious violence is a disease spreading through our communities, infecting our young people'.

The portrayal of butchery as a contagious illness reveals an official mindset that treats dangerous offenders as victims of society, devoid of responsibility for their actions, and in need of support rather than punishment.

Forty per cent of criminals caught more than once in possession of a knife are spared jail.

The average custodial term for carrying an offensive weapon is just 7.5 months.

Only a third of criminals convicted of violent offences are imprisoned.

Criminals can commit up to 60 offences before prison

The Daily Telegraph, 4th January 2020

The number of criminals with more than 50 previous convictions spared prison sentences in 2018 triples the total for 2007.

Note: This lays bare the justice system's increased leniency towards criminals and makes a lie of the propaganda that says British courts send too many offenders to prison.

What does it take to get locked up?

The Daily Mail, 22nd August 2018

Thugs guilty of despicably violent crimes are free to walk the streets thanks to our spineless courts.

Three jailed over Park Lane bouncer's death

The Daily Telegraph, 28th March 2020

Three men attacked Tudor Simionov, 33, when he went to help a colleague working on the door of a club in Park Lane. Mr Simionov was stabbed fatally in the chest, and five other members of staff were injured.

All three admitted manslaughter and were sentenced as follows:

Adam Khalil, 21: 11 years

Haroon Akram, 26: six years and nine months

Barber Nor Hamada, 24: seven years

Note: *Due to remission, Khalil will serve no more than 7.4 years; Akram and Hamada, no more than 4.5 years each. They will all still be young when released.*

Brothers in Evil

The Daily Mail, 18th March 2020

On 17th March 2020, Hashem Abedi, 22, the brother of the Manchester suicide bomber, was found guilty of 22 murders.

BBC News Online, 20th August 2020

On 20th August 2020, Hashem Abedi was sentenced to life imprisonment with a minimum tariff of 55 years.
Men, women and children were among those killed, and hundreds of others were injured by the explosion at Manchester Arena on 22nd May 2017.

Note: *A minimum tariff of 55 years for 22 murders equates to 2.5 years per murder to be served before parole can be considered. How many does one need to kill to receive a full life sentence?*

Teenage paedophile jailed for raping girl, 11

The Daily Telegraph, 8th June 2013

In January 2013, 18-year-old Opemipo Jaji was sentenced to an 18-month supervision order for making indecent images of children.

He had previously sexually assaulted and robbed a 12-year-old girl.

Six months later, on 7th June 2013, he was sentenced to a minimum of eight years' imprisonment for raping an 11-year-old girl.

He had just left his probation officer when he saw the child going home from school. He followed her and dragged her into a park and subjected her to a three-hour ordeal.

More than 50,000 drug offenders escape with a 'slap on the wrist'

Digital Telegraph, 2019

During 2019, 130,000 community resolution orders (CROs) were made against offenders, as an alternative to a formal sentence.

Community Resolution Order:

This allows the offender to avoid a criminal record.
The offender 'resolves' the offence by apologising to the victim or paying compensation.

Thirty-one thousand CROs, almost a third of the total, were used in relation to violent offences.

Overall, the proportion of crimes resulting in an offender being charged has fallen to a record low of 7%.

It is probable that the figure of 7% refers to recorded crime.

60% of serious offenders are let off with a caution

MailOnline, 24th December 2007

Some police forces are letting off six out of ten serious offenders with a caution.

Instead of hauling the violent attackers before court, officers desperate to meet Whitehall targets simply give them a 'slap on the wrist'.

The Bully's Charter: Boy given target of seven assaults a week

The Daily Mail, 22nd April 1995

A foul-mouthed ten-year-old boy who attacked 14 classmates in less than a week was allowed back into lessons provided he promised to hit only half as many.

This thug's charter was drawn up by a Northumberland educational psychologist.

Huge fall in criminals sent to prison

The Sunday Times, 5th January 1997

A criminal is five times less likely to be jailed today than in 1950.

Triple child killer to go free

The Sun, 4th December 2018

In 1973, David McGreavy beat to death Samantha, aged nine months, strangled her brother, Paul, aged four years, and cut the throat of sister, Dawn, aged two years.

He then mutilated their bodies with a pickaxe before impaling them on garden railings.

He was given a life sentence with a minimum tariff of 20 years.

In November 2018, the Parole Board ordered his release.

The children's mother, Elsie Urry, said, 'I was told he would never go free.'

A Green Light For Criminals

The Daily Mail, 27th June 2018

Anger as Justice Minister Rory Stewart calls for most sentences of less than a year to be axed to cut jail population.

He even claimed that victims of crime would be 'better off' with fewer criminals in jail.

Tens of thousands commit a new crime within a month of receiving a caution

MailOnline, 21st January 2012

Figures published in 2011 showed the police handed out cautions to 235,600 thugs instead of passing the cases to prosecutors to administer justice in the courts.

Within a month, 21,000 of them had been reconvicted (almost 10%).

Within twelve months, over 125,000 of them had been reconvicted (53%).

Every year, hundreds of adult criminals receive cautions despite having been convicted of offences more than 15 times.

Thousands of those with at least 15 previous convictions when they were cautioned go on to receive another caution within a year.

Note: *The figure of 53% quoted above for cautioned offenders reconvicted within 12 months hides more than it reveals. It is based on just **one** court appearance made in the 12 months from the date of the caution. Many offenders will have made **several court** appearances during this time.*

It is normal for offenders to be charged with several offences at each court appearance. Most crimes are never cleared up, so their true reoffending rate will be much higher, and likely to be nearer 100%. This is the case for all offenders placed under some form of community supervision.

Government figures show over 200,000 offences were dealt with by caution and other out-of-court methods in 2020, a quarter of which were for violent crimes.

Thug Given Freedom to Wreck a Life

MailOnline, 21st January 2012

Adam Smith, 25, escaped with a police caution after knocking a man unconscious in an unprovoked attack in a nightclub queue.

Within months, he was handed a second police caution after punching another man.

A year later, in November 2011, he left another victim, Phillip Snowden, with devastating injuries after kicking his head like a football. Mr Snowden was left permanently disabled, unable to walk or talk again.

Note: *Judge Christopher Batty expressed 'disbelief' at the caution previously handed to the attacker. How should we react to the nine-year prison sentence he then handed down to Smith? The judge would have known that because of automatic remission, Smith would serve no more than 4.5 years for an offence for which a whole-life term of imprisonment would not have been unjust.*

Soft Justice for Repeat Offenders

The Daily Telegraph, 13th April 2013

One in three offenders who breaches conditions attached to a caution escapes further punishment, figures from the Crown Prosecution Service show.

Scores of rapists and killers allowed home on bail after they are convicted

The Daily Mail, 19th March 2015

My jail time for thug is pathetic, says judge

The Daily Telegraph, 13th October 2012

An unprovoked attack left Matthew Edmonds, 33, paralysed from the neck down.

His attacker, Samuel Evans, 21, was already subject to a suspended jail term for a previous assault, when he lashed out at Mr Edmonds.

Evans was convicted of grievous bodily harm and jailed for a total of 34 months.

The judge complained that sentencing guidelines did not allow him to pass a longer term or one that would truly mark the gravity of the offence.

Note: *In the same month that Evans was sentenced, a mother in Texas who beat and kicked her two-year-old daughter and glued her hands to a wall was sentenced to 99 years in jail.*

I have never seen anything so wet in all my life

Bristol Evening Post, 28th January 2011

Judge Lambert told a burglar, 'I very much regret sentencing guidelines which say I should not send you straight to prison.'

He complained that for a burglary, his sentence of 240 hours of community work (plus a curfew order and 18 months' supervision) was too lenient.

Note: *Daniel Rogers was convicted of burglary in Bristol in September 2010. He had been caught red-handed by the homeowner. A probation officer's report had recommended a non-custodial sentence, to which the judge replied: 'I have never seen anything so wet in all my life.'*

Violent burglars could still be spared jail terms

The Daily Telegraph, 12th March 2010

Sentencing advice from the Sentencing Advisory Panel allows judges:

To avoid prison for burglary, even if the burglar broke into a home containing children

or used violence

or was armed

or left their victim particularly traumatised.

Courts were also given the option to consider community penalties for the burglar if he was 'drug' dependent.

Note: *Figures for January 2010 showed that a householder was attacked by a burglar the equivalent of every 30 minutes in England and Wales.*

At Liberty to Kill and Rape

Criminals left free to murder

The Daily Mail, 2nd July 1997

A Home Office inquiry revealed that every week at least one freed criminal under probation supervision is charged with murder.

Fury as thug who kicked WPC in front of bus gets just 3 and a half years imprisonment

The Daily Mail, 22nd January 2019

Two criminals, Kersan Euell, 20, and Martin Payne, 19, attacked two police officers in a bid to escape, having been pulled over for a routine stop.

Euell karate kicked WPC McGinty in the head and pushed her into the path of a bus.

Payne dragged PC Collins across the road and threatened him with a knife.

Both officers were seriously injured.

Payne did not have a licence or insurance for the BMW he was driving. Both Payne and Euell were on post-release licence from prison.

Sentencing Kersan Euell for actual bodily harm, Judge Sarah Plaschkes said, 'Euell should have faced more serious charges.'

The Crown Prosecution Service had reduced the charge from grievous bodily harm to actual bodily harm.

Note: *The maximum penalty for actual bodily harm is five years; for grievous bodily harm it is life imprisonment.*

Four years for man who killed shopper in supermarket row

The Guardian, 2nd April 2009

Tony Virasami, 38, who had been called into a supermarket by his former partner to deal with a row, killed Kevin Tripp, 57, by punching him to the ground.

But Tripp had not been involved. Antoinette Richardson had rowed with Adam Prendergast, who had pushed in front of her in the queue.

As Tripp lay bloodied and unmoving, she was heard to say: 'We need to find the right guy.'

Virasami, a career criminal with many convictions, including for violence, pleaded not guilty to manslaughter but was convicted.

The judge passed a four-year prison sentence on Virasami.

Tripp's brother described the sentence as 'a sad reflection on the British judicial system'.

Tripp's partner said: 'It's not long enough. They took Kevin's life.'

Note: *The judge said: 'An entirely innocent man has lost his life, and his family have lost him forever.' He also said it would have been bad enough if Virasami had got the right man, thereby accepting that there was a right man to get.*

Court let youth, 17, go free to rape

The Daily Express, 4th June 2008

A pregnant woman was beaten and raped by a disturbed teenager a day after magistrates freed him.

They had been told by psychiatrists that the youth was dangerous and should be locked up.

The court let him go because they were told there was no secure hospital place for him.

Within hours, he unleashed his attack on a 20-year-old woman who was four months' pregnant.

The offender had 43 previous convictions, many for violence.

Parole rules 'put freed criminals ahead of victims'

The Daily Mail, 1st August 2013

Victims of crime not allowed to see updated photographs of their attackers.

Child killer's sentence cut by five years

The Daily Telegraph, 9th October 2002

Steven Leisk, 39, abducted a nine-year-old boy, Scott Simpson, from a park and strangled him to death.

His body was left in the grounds of the nearby university in Glasgow.

Leisk was on a prison-release licence at the time, following previous attacks on children.

His life sentence with a minimum tariff of 25 years was reviewed and reduced to 20 years.

Scott's parents said they were horrified by the ruling.

Serial rapist freed from jail to strike again

The Daily Express, 8th July 2009

Alexander McArthur was sentenced to life imprisonment in 1994 for raping and attempting to kill a woman.

Yet 40-year-old McArthur was released on licence after serving ten years.

Following this, in November 2008, he subjected another woman to a horrific seven-hour knifepoint ordeal.

He was sentenced to a minimum term of 20 years' imprisonment.

Teenage criminals to get one caution for multiple offences

The Daily Telegraph, 7th March 2009

Spared jail, mum who threw her baby son at policewoman

The Daily Mail, 3rd December 2019

Kirsty Bearfield, a bare-knuckle fighter from Hull, threw her 15-month-old son at DC Kirsty Burnett.

Bearfield had just been told that the baby boy and his elder brother would have to stay with his father due to concerns over an injury to the older child.

The policewoman caught the 30lb baby but seriously injured her neck in an attempt to ensure the child was not hurt. As a result, her mobility is now significantly restricted, and this has affected both her work and her private life.

Bearfield was convicted of grievous bodily harm. She had four previous convictions for battery.

The judge said he did not think he could pass an immediate prison sentence as the offence had occurred two years earlier. He imposed a 12-month suspended sentence instead.

Note: *This is an example of what occurs almost daily in British courts. Concerns for the criminal take precedence over all else.*

Stephen Chafer jailed for life after stabbing dementia sufferer

The Daily Telegraph, 5th January 2019

1979: Chafer was jailed for life for raping and murdering three-year-old Lorraine Holt near her home in Derby.

2002: released.

2013: returned to prison after he torched his neighbour's flat.

2017: released again.

2018: he battered and stabbed Mrs Fay Mills, and tried to kill her neighbour, Mark Patchett, who came to her assistance.

2019: he was sentenced to life imprisonment with a minimum tariff of 17 years.

Note: *What must this criminal do for the courts to decide he must be imprisoned for the rest of his life?*

Killer freed early blinded woman after she refused him cigarette

The Daily Telegraph, 19th January 2008

September 2005: Nicholas Hague admitted manslaughter.

He was jailed for 18 months.

He was released early (after serving nine months).

Several months later, he launched a horrific attack on 60-year-old Susan Collins, because she refused to give him a cigarette.

He kicked her to the ground and repeatedly stamped on her face.

His victim needed to be put on a life support machine.

She needed surgery to remove a blood clot from between her skull and her brain.

The attack left her blind in one eye.

At Warrington Crown Court, Hague was sentenced to an indeterminate term of imprisonment for public protection (IPP). He was given a minimum tariff of three years and five months, to be served before parole could be considered.

Note. *IPPs were introduced for violent and dangerous criminals who posed a serious threat to the public. But the protection element was undermined by the short minimum tariffs given by judges in many of these cases.*

Indeterminate Sentences for Public Protection (IPP)

Introduced in 2003 for those convicted of dangerous violent and sex crimes, who were judged to pose a risk of further harm.

Government data published in 2013 revealed that 70% of IPPs were given minimum tariffs of less than four years.

They were abolished in December 2012.

Wanted thug let into Britain to strike again

The Daily Express, 14th March 2008

Damian Brauer, 21, a Polish robber on the run from jail in his own country, entered Britain by slipping past border control officials.

During an altercation, he stabbed 19-year-old Matthew Buckman ten times in the neck and back.

Ipswich Crown Court passed an Indeterminate Sentence for Public Protection, with a minimum tariff of 27 months.

Note: *When Brauer had served 27 months, the Parole Board would have had to decide when to release him. This would be based on their guess as to whether he was 'safe enough' to let out. The low minimum tariff set by the judge could not but send a strong message about how serious he considered the crime and the level of threat Brauer posed to the public.*

Murderer of Jacqueline Ross sentenced to life imprisonment with a minimum tariff of 22 years

Macclesfield Express, 30th November 2005

Ben Redfern-Edwards, 21, was released after serving only half of his sentence for a violent robbery.

On 30th January 2005, within 72 hours of being let out of prison, he battered to death 44-year-old Jacqueline Ross, whose path he had crossed by chance, 'because her dog had barked at him'.

When her body was found, it was discovered she had sustained horrific head injuries inflicted with a rock.

He was sentenced to life imprisonment with a tariff of 22 years. The judge reduced the sentence because of his age and also because the attack was instantaneous and not premeditated.

Note: *While the family of Jacqueline Ross and everyone else viewed her killing as the most heinous of crimes, the judge offered them the consolation that it would have been very much worse if Redfern-Edwards had planned her death beforehand.*

Freed robber obsessed with the rich guilty of stabbing financier to death

The Guardian, 16th December 2005

In 1998, Damien Hanson, 17, was convicted of attempted murder with a machete while robbing a man of his Rolex watch.

He was sentenced to 12 years' imprisonment.

In 2004, he was released after serving seven years.

Three months later, he murdered John Monckton, 49, and attempted to murder his wife, Homeyra, 46, while robbing them in their home in Chelsea.

He was sentenced to life imprisonment with a tariff of 36 years.

Damien Hanson (continued)
Previous criminal history and
sentences received

Guardian, 16th December 2005
and
HM Inspectorate of Probation, Serious Further Offence Review,
February 2006

3rd February 1993: indecent assault, six-month supervision order

6th September 1993: theft, fined

3rd May 1995: assault and theft, compensation order

July 1995: burglary, conditional discharge

August 1996: unlawful wounding and contempt, 18 months'
detention

1997: attempted burglary, four months' imprisonment

1998: attempted murder, 12 years' imprisonment

2004: released after serving seven years

Note: *His previous sentencing record is typical of the inconsistency and
leniency shown by the Parole Board and courts throughout Britain.*

Roy Whiting, Child Killer

The Daily Telegraph, 15th November 2001
and
Today, BBC Radio 4, 16th December 2001:
Interview with the sentencing judge of Roy Whiting

4th March 1995: Roy Whiting was convicted of the abduction and sexual assault of an eight-year-old girl.

He was sentenced to four years' imprisonment.

He was released in November 1997, after serving two years and five months of his sentence.

Three years later, he abducted and murdered eight-year-old Sarah Payne.

Note: *The public were astonished to learn of the lenient four-year sentence he received for the earlier abduction and sexual assault of a child. (The maximum sentence allowed for this crime is life imprisonment.)*

In an interview on the Today programme, the judge responsible said:
'The public must realise there is a limit to the punishment which can be exacted against a criminal. The sentence of four years was in line with the Court of Appeal guidelines at the time.'

Day Release from Prison

Prisoners are allowed out on day release to help them prepare for their life in the community following their final discharge from prison.

The following are four examples of how some prisoners use this privilege.

All these prisoners would have been assessed by psychologists and probation staff as suitable candidates for these periods of temporary release, and thus safe to let out.

Day-release rapist Alan Wilmot given further life sentences

BBC News, 25th June 2015

In 1987, Wilmot, then 21, was convicted of robbing and raping four women in West London. He was sentenced to life imprisonment.

In 2004, on the recommendation of the Parole Board, he was transferred to an open prison as preparation for his release.

Within a year, he had to be returned to secure conditions because of his 'inappropriate behaviour'.

Despite being overruled by the government on several occasions, the Parole Board made repeated attempts to get him returned to open conditions, and finally achieved this in 2015.

During day release, he raped a 27-year-old woman at knifepoint in front of a close friend who was forced to watch the ordeal.

He was later convicted of these new crimes and given another four life sentences.

Note: *All is not as it seems. Despite being given five life sentences, he will be eligible for parole in 2030. All his life terms are to run <u>concurrently</u>, and he was given a tariff of 15 years.*

Inmate robs bank during day release

The Daily Telegraph, 17th September 2011

Micquel Daniel France, 24, was sentenced to 12 years' imprisonment for attempted murder in March 2006.

In May 2011, while out on day release from Sudbury Prison in Derbyshire, he robbed a Barclays Bank in Powys.

Murderer raided betting shops on day release

The Daily Telegraph, 20th September 2011

In 1997, Joseph Williams, then 38, was sentenced to life imprisonment for murder.

In 2011, while out on day release from Blantyre House prison in Kent, he raided several betting shops.

He was convicted of eight charges of robbery, three attempted robberies and nine charges of possessing an imitation firearm.

Mrs Buck criticises the release system

The Bucks Herald, 24th March 2015

The failures that let murderer Ian McLoughlin out on day release to kill again.

The Daily Mail, 24th March 2015
and
MailOnline, 21st October 2013

Victim 1
1984: Ian McLoughlin killed his fist victim. Given ten years for manslaughter.

Victim 2
Released early and in 1992 he stabbed his landlord to death. He was given a 'life' sentence with a 25-year tariff.
After 21 years in prison, his preparation for release began. He was allowed several temporary releases from prison, despite often breaking the rules.

Victim 3
In July 2013, while on day release yet again from Springfield Prison, he murdered 66-year-old Graham Buck, who had gone to the aid of his neighbour, 87-year-old Frances Cory White, whose house McLoughlin was burgling.
McLoughlin was sentenced to his second 'life' sentence with a tariff of 40 years. A ruling by the European Court had prevented the judge from sending him to prison for the rest of his life.

An Appeal by the Attorney General to the British Appeal Court changed the sentence to a whole-life term.

McLoughlin's sister said he had always been violent. 'He should have been hanged for what he has done.'

Note: *This is a case of a whole-life term being given 21 years too late.*

Killing a man? It's no big deal

The Daily Mail, 27th February 2014

Lewis Gill, a violent and convicted robber, killed Andrew Young, aged 40, with a single punch.

Mr Young had done no more than challenge a friend of Gill for riding his bicycle on the pavement.

Gill was convicted of manslaughter.

Andrew Young's mother was astonished at the court's sentence of just four years in jail.

She was further stunned to learn that due to remission, Gill would be released automatically at the halfway stage and spend no more than two years behind bars.

The Court of Appeal later upheld the sentence, saying it was 'not unduly lenient'.

Note: *If the Appeal judges think that two years behind bars is long enough for killing someone, what would a criminal have to do for them to pass a longer sentence?*

UK-based Kurdish ISIS fanatic who urged German Jihadi terror cell to commit mass murder with a car, bomb and meat cleaver is jailed for life

The Daily Mail, 26th June 2020

Fatah Abdullah, who had been granted asylum in Britain, was sentenced to two life sentences by a British court, with a minimum tariff of just *nine years.*

Teenager livestreamed stabbing his dad in 'premeditated and brutal attack'

WalesOnline, 24th July 2020

A 17-year-old attacked his father with a knife and stabbed him several times in the neck and chest.

The judge said to film and broadcast the attack was 'chilling'.

He sentenced the youth to two years' imprisonment.

Note: *Of significance is the fact that the judge described the filming of the teenager's attack as chilling – not the attack itself.*

Blunders that left crazed rapist free to attack 11 victims

The Daily Mail, 30th January 2020

Serial rapist Joseph McCann was imprisoned for burglary in 2017 and freed in February 2019.

Following his release, probation officers missed several opportunities to have him recalled.

This allowed him to kidnap, rape and sexually assault 11 women and children, aged 11 to 71.

In December 2019, he was given 33 life terms of imprisonment.

But they were all *concurrent,* which meant in reality he had been given one life term.

Note: *Despite committing crimes for which a whole-life term would not have been unjust, the prison door still remains ajar for McCann. His 30-year tariff means, despite the judge's theatrical flourish in pretending to give him '33 life terms', that he can apply for parole in 2050. The record of the Parole Board gives little room to think they will want to keep him locked up after that point. McCann will then be 65 years old and still potentially dangerous.*

Drug Dealer Birmingham mechanic spared jail – despite 60 offences

The Birmingham Mail, 30th October 2019

Calvin Downing, 35, a drug dealer, was spared jail after committing a staggering 60 offences, many related to the supply of drugs.

On 22nd November 2018, police pulled him over and found significant quantities of drugs in his car.

He had no licence, having already been banned from driving for driving while disqualified.

The West Midlands court found him guilty of possession with intent to supply Class B drugs. The judge was told Downing had previously appeared in the dock 21 times charged with 59 offences.

He was given a ten-month prison sentence, *suspended* for 18 months. He was also ordered to complete 80 hours' unpaid work and 15 days of rehabilitation activity.

Note: *Lenient sentencing such as this leaves little room for doubt as to why criminals such as Downing are prepared to carry on offending. These pretend punishments make their criminal activities worth the risk.*

Executive jailed for £3m fraud

The Daily Telegraph, 27th June 2020

Simon Oliver, 42, stole almost £3 million from his employers, Crédit Industriel et Commercial bank, by setting up two fake payments to himself.

Southwark Crown Court imprisoned him for four and a half years.

Note: *With remission, he will serve 27 months in prison. This means that for every £111,000 he stole, he will spend one month in jail.*

Only one in 14 crimes solved amid surge in knife offences

The Daily Telegraph, 18th July 2020

Comparisons of the proportion of other crimes solved for 2019/20 with those solved in 2013/14 were:

For rape, 1.4% compared with 8.5% in 2014

For violent offences, it was 6.9% compared with 22%

For robbery, 7.2% compared with 17.3%

For thefts, 5.2% compared with 10.8%

For drug offences, 23.9% compared with 33%

For public order offences, 8.4% compared with 31.4%

For weapons possessions, 8.4% compared with 31.4%

Note: *These disturbingly low numbers of crimes solved amount to a form of institutionalised leniency. They are indicators of a justice system that neither delineates right from wrong, nor protects the public. Again, the figures probably relate to recorded crime.*

Mairead Philpott killed her six children after burning down their family home in Derby

MailOnline, 30th November 2020
and
ITV News, Derby, 29th November 2020

Mick Philpott led his wife, Mairead, in what was a scheme to get a bigger council house, by burning his Derby home and framing his ex-lover Lisa Willis for the crime.

He intended to rescue the children but the plan went wrong and the blaze claimed the lives of six of their 17 children, by smoke inhalation.

They wept at a press conference and appealed for help to find the killer or killers of the children, aged five to 13, who died in the blaze. But their later behaviour aroused suspicion and they were subsequently charged.

Mick Philpott was sentenced to life imprisonment for the manslaughter of six of their children and given a minimum tariff of 15 years.

Mairead Philpott was convicted of the manslaughter of six of their children and sentenced to 17 years' imprisonment.

Mairead was released in November 2020, after serving seven and a half years (less than half her sentence).

Note: *The judge described the crime as 'a wicked and dangerous plan, beyond the comprehension of any right-thinking person'. Is this not also true of the decision to release Mairead Philpott? The local MP said: 'She should have been given a life sentence for every child lost, and never come out.'*

Rape 'has been decriminalised'. Watchdog's damning claim as number of cases taken to trial plunges by 52%

The Daily Mail, 14th July 2020

Victims' Commissioner Dame Vera Baird blasted prosecutors for shocking failures in the way they handle rape crime.

Just 1,758 rape cases were taken to trial in the year ending March 2019. This is a 52% drop on the previous year.

She said that because so few cases were prosecuted, sex predators know they are 'highly unlikely to be held to account'.

Note: *This last observation is true of crime generally.*

Numbers jailed for knife crimes fall

MailOnline, 16th January 2020

According to Ministry of Justice figures, more than a third of repeat knife offenders escape an immediate jail sentence.

This is despite laws which require courts to impose a custodial sentence for anyone convicted of a second subsequent offence involving, using or possessing a knife.

Knife teens could be spared jail if they are from 'troubled homes'

The Daily Mail, 6th October 2016

This is a Sentencing Advisory Panel Direction

Note: *Many of the directions from the sentencing advisory panel undermine legislation passed by Parliament, as illustrated by the example above.*

The Crime and Sentencing Act came into force in December 1999 (It introduced the 'three-strikes' sentencing rule)

Its effect was that criminals with two previous court appearances, each of which carried a conviction for burglary, who were convicted for burglary at a third court appearance should be sentenced to a mandatory minimum period of three years' imprisonment.

Three strikes rule fails to jail a single burglar

The Mail on Sunday, 2nd June 2002

In the year-long period from 1st December 1999 (when the three-strikes rule came into force) to January 2001, there were no mandatory sentences passed on domestic burglars.

Yet in this period there were almost half a million of these crimes committed in England and Wales.

In the two-year period between 1st December 1999 and 31st December 2001, there were 840,000 domestic burglaries recorded for England and Wales. Once again, not one burglar was jailed under the three-strikes rule.

The Home Secretary instructed his officials not to pass on this information to anyone, and these figures remained hidden until June 2002, when they were finally leaked to the press.

Note: *Almost 20 years later, nothing has changed, as the following headline shows. The courts remain determined to protect burglars from just punishment.*

Why?

Judges fail to enforce '3-strikes' law for burglars

The Daily Telegraph, 8th August 2020

About 75% of serial house robbers get off with less than the mandatory three-year sentence.

This means thousands escape the minimum three-year period of imprisonment for their 'third strike', and are given suspended sentences or community punishments.

This is despite courts being instructed by the Lord Chief Justice to hand out tough jail sentences for burglars, because the home should be a person's 'safest refuge'.

Five months after this instruction was given, the Sentencing Advisory Panel advised the courts that burglars could avoid jail if they were drug addicts or alcoholics.

The three-strikes Deceit

Although resisted by many in the justice system as being overpunitive, the three-year mandatory prison sentence for burglars is excessively lenient.

The three-strike rule operates on the third court appearance for burglary, not the third burglary conviction.

By the third court appearance, the average burglar would have committed scores of these crimes, most of which are never brought to court.

Due to 50% remission, the three-year sentence means no more than18 months served.

Rapist jailed for **29** years for murder of childhood friend

The Daily Telegraph, 8th August 2020

On 7th August 2020, at Stafford Crown Court, Wesley Streete, 20, was convicted of:

The rape and murder of 20-year-old Keeley Bunker

Two separate counts of rape against other women

Three counts of sexual assault against other women

He was sentenced to life imprisonment for the murder and rape with a minimum tariff of 29 years.

He was sentenced to jail terms of between six months and five years for the other five offences.

All seven sentences are to run concurrently.

Note: *In summary, this means he was sentenced to just over four years per offence before parole can be considered.*

24-year-old man threw 5-month-old baby at a TV cabinet

The Daily Mail, 23rd June 2020

On 29th October 2019, Taylor Biggins threw a five-month-old baby at a television. He lost his temper when the baby was crying.

The child suffered a fractured skull and permanent brain damage, as well as other associated injuries, including damage to his retina.

On 23rd June 2020, Leeds Crown Court sentenced him to two years and ten months' imprisonment.

Note: 50% automatic release means he will serve no more than one year and five months.

If two-thirds remission is applied, he will serve no more than one year and nine months, as punishment for a crime justly deserving a much longer period of imprisonment.

The newspaper report discussed Taylor's 'problems' at length but made no reference to the leniency of the sentence, or the long-term impact his crime will have on the baby boy's development.

Teenager who murdered young footballer is jailed

The Daily Telegraph, 10th October 2020

Sukhbir Phull, 18, was convicted in September 2020 of murdering 16-year-old Ramani Morgan, outside a house party in Coventry on 29th February.

Morgan died from a wound to the heart.

Sukhbir Phull was sentenced to life imprisonment with a tariff of 17 years.

Note: *Once again, the terrible crime of murder is not matched by the punishment. If released in 17 years, Phull will be only 35.*

Trio who 'scalped' trainee nurse by ripping her hair out by roots avoid jail

The Daily Telegraph, 17th October 2020

Donna Goulding, 25, Chloe Cummings, 29, and Toni Tyler, 30, violently attacked a trainee nurse, Hollie-Louise Brown, outside a nightspot in Ashington.

They ripped her hair out in a ferocious attack, and were described as 'behaving like a pack of animals'.

All three were convicted of causing an affray.

Cummings and Tyler were given 12-month community orders, with 80 hours' work.

Goulding was given a suspended 13-month jail term, plus 80 hours of community work.

The judge, Edward Bindloss, said: 'I have to be realistic, you are all single mothers.'

Note: *It could be argued that being single mothers makes their crime worse, so justifying a severe punishment. Being single mothers did not stop them committing a violent crime at a nightspot.*

Burnley 'role model' attacker gets suspended sentence

The Lancashire Telegraph, 16th March 2011

Apprentice plumber and youth worker, Nathan Jackson, 18, attacked a 17-year-old, leaving him with a broken nose, broken cheekbone and broken eye socket.

He was convicted of grievous bodily harm and given 13 months in custody, suspended for 12 months.

Note: *Another example of a 'pretend' sentence for a crime for which the perpetrator could have received a life sentence.*

Peckham teen who raped and imprisoned 18-year-old woman jailed for five years

The Evening Standard, 10th November 2020

Tamoy Bailey was 16 when he imprisoned and raped an 18-year-old woman at an address in Peckham, London, in March 2019.

He threatened her with a knife and said he would stab her if she did not have sex with him.

On 2nd November 2020, Bailey (then 18) was sentenced to five years' imprisonment for the rape and three years to run concurrently for the false imprisonment.

The judge described him as representing a 'significant risk of harm to the public'.

The police described him as an 'arrogant, violent sexual offender who thought he could get away with raping this young woman'.

The practical effect of his concurrent sentence is that he was given five years in total for both offences.

Note: *If the two-thirds remission rule operates, he will serve three years and four months, and only two and a half years if the 50% remission rule operates, for committing two of the most serious violent crimes on the statute book.*

Man jailed for setting fire to police officers

The Daily Telegraph, 7th November 2020

Blagovest Hadjigueorguiev, 30, doused two police officers with petrol as they assisted with an eviction in September 2020.

PC Mares was engulfed by flames and sustained severe burns to his legs and left hand. PC Alan Lenton was also injured by the flames.

Hadjigueorguiev was sentenced to ten years and six months' imprisonment.

Note: *If the 50% remission rule operates, he will serve just over five years for a crime that threatened the lives of two police officers, or seven years if the two-thirds remission rule is used.*

If the two-thirds rule operates, this represents three and a half years for each of the officers he set alight. If the 50% rule is used, it means he will serve just over two and a half years for each of the officers who were burned.

Manchester police 'ignore one in five crimes'

The Daily Telegraph, 10th December 2020

The figure is similar for violent crimes.
Police Inspectorate said that the current situation was wholly
unacceptable.

Greater Manchester Police failed to record 80,000 crimes in 12-month period (2019/20)

Manchester Evening News, 10th December 2020

Note: *The tone of the article and the Police Inspectorate's response suggests this failure is a new problem and is localised to one area.*

Nothing could be further from the truth, as illustrated by the following eight examples.

Police who give up on half of crimes

The Daily Mail, 24th April 2019

The *Mail* found that other forces (such as Wiltshire and Bedfordshire) also failed to investigate large numbers of crimes, blaming funding cuts.

Police 'write off a third of crimes'

The Daily Telegraph, 1st June 2011

Figures obtained from a number of police forces (such as West Yorkshire, the Metropolitan Police, and Devon and Cornwall) showed that in 2010 they ignored hundreds of thousands of crimes, including violent and sex attacks.

Violent crimes are being ignored by police, says report

The Independent, 22nd October 2009

The Police Inspectorate report estimated that thousands of violent crimes are being ignored.

Law Breaking View is Strange

The Bristol Post, 25th June 2013

Chief constable admits he ignores hundreds of 'low-level' crimes.

Police 'encouraged to reclassify crimes to keep numbers down'

Metro, 4th April 2011

An anonymous police officer, 'Inspector Gadget', revealed that the police routinely ignore hundreds of crimes and reclassify others, in order to keep the numbers down.

We regularly fiddle crime numbers, admit police

The Times, 20th November 2013

Evidence given to the Commons Public Administration Select Committee revealed methods used by the police to massage crime figures.
MPs were appalled to hear how crime numbers are falsified and serious crimes 'downgraded'.

Police failing to record one in five crimes

The Daily Mail, 1st May 2014

A report by the Police Inspectorate (HMIC, 30th April 2014) revealed that the police are failing to record 20% of crimes.

As a result, up to 740,000 victims of violence, burglary and other offences are denied the most minimal justice.

One in five crimes not recorded by police

The Daily Mail, 18th November 2014

A Police Inspectorate report (HMIC, 18th November 2014) revealed that the police fail to record more than 800,000 crimes every year, including thousands of violent and sex crimes.

50,000 crooks dodge going to court

The Daily Mail, 1st May 2014

In 2013, around 400,000 crimes were dealt with by means of a police caution. These included violent crimes, drug use and other offences.

However, inspectors found that in one in every seven cases, it had been wrong to issue a caution. This allowed 50,000 criminals with long histories of law breaking to escape without any punishment.

Attack by two violent teenagers leaves the victim in vegetative state

MailOnline, 21st March 2020

In February 2020, 19-year-old Keiano Gooden-Josephs and a 17-year-old co-attacker assaulted a 21-year-old man with machetes.

The attack took place in Preston Park, Wembley, in full view of the public. They hacked at their victim with such force that he was left in a permanent vegetative state.

Gooden-Josephs was sentenced to 13 years' imprisonment for GBH, and the 17-year-old attacker was sentenced to 11 years' imprisonment.

Note: *Due to remission, Gooden-Josephs will serve no more than eight years and eight months, and his co-attacker just over seven years, for an assault in which their victim was stabbed so forcibly in the chest that he was left brain dead and is likely to die. They will be 27 and 22 years old respectively when released.*

Half of all gun criminals avoid minimum jail term

The Daily Telegraph, 18th October 2008

Ministry of Justice figures show that in 2006 only 141 out of 281 sentenced for possession of a firearm received the mandatory minimum of five years' imprisonment.

and

Criminals get licence to carry on shooting

Simon Heffer writes:

The law-abiding public live in trepidation of losing their firearm licence, and slavishly adhere to the rules, many of them nit-picking.

Why is it that serious criminals are treated so leniently while those with no criminal intent are given such a hard time?

Is it because it is easier to prosecute the harmless than to prosecute the harmful?

Jail 'not useful' for attack youth

The Daily Telegraph, 2nd October 2010

A teenager attacked 26-year-old Nicholas Butt, leaving him severely paralysed and able to communicate only by blinking.

The judge ruled that prison 'would not be useful' as the attacker would only have received eight months' imprisonment. He was instead given a supervision order.

Attacker walks free while another jailed

The Bristol Evening Post, 5th January 2011

Nineteen-year-old Jamie Smith punched and kicked Robert Andrews in Bristol on 8th November 2010. The attack was unprovoked. At one point, he was seen stamping on Mr Andrew's head.

He was convicted of assault and occasioning actual bodily harm at Bristol Crown Court and was jailed for three months.

In another courtroom, Daniel Phillips, 20, was found guilty of causing grievous bodily harm. He knocked Peter Davies, 42, to the ground and tried to stamp on him. He left Mr Davies unconscious and motionless on the ground, outside a Bristol nightclub on 30th May 2010.

Judge Hagen sentenced him to a 12-month jail term, suspended for 18 months.

One of the reasons she gave for this exceptional leniency was the 'recent death of his mother'.

Phillips was later seen celebrating wildly in the court corridor with his friends.

Two thirds of violent criminals avoid jail

The Daily Telegraph, 27th June 2009

Only one in three violent criminals is jailed.

Dominic Grieve, the shadow justice secretary, said: 'It adds insult to injury that two thirds of violent offenders are being let off with a slap on the wrist.'

By way of contrast, the following is a report from the United States.

Politician confronts gunman who failed to kill her

The Daily Telegraph, 9th November 2012

In 2011, former congresswoman Gabrielle Giffords was one of 13 people shot down in a mass shooting in Tuscon, Arizona. She was shot through the head at close range but survived. Six other people were killed.

Jared Loughner, 24, was convicted of murder and attempted murder and sentenced to seven *consecutive* life terms of imprisonment *without* parole.

Note: *In the 1980s, the US introduced more severe sentencing for violent and other criminals. Their crime rate for violent and other offences is now half of what it was then.*

We return to Britain:

Police force that can't attend every 999 call but can run a dog blog

The Daily Telegraph, 5th February 2010

A chief constable claimed her force could not attend every emergency call because of lack of resources.

Yet it can afford to feature blogs on its website 'written' by police dogs.

Surely the police have got better things to do ...

The Daily Express, 9th June 2009

Police were seen hiding behind a beach hut, using speed cameras to catch cyclists travelling at more than 10 mph along a Bournemouth beachfront promenade.

Up to 400,000 police records wiped out in IT blunder

The Daily Telegraph, 16th January 2021

Criminals freed by 'worrying' rate of court mistakes

The Daily Telegraph, 24th October 2009

Crimes 'cover-up' by court

The Daily Express, 12th March 2008

Police lose contact with over 400 offenders on the Sex Offender Register

The Daily Mail, 11th March 2015

CPS? It stands for Couldn't Prosecute Satan, says police sergeant

The Daily Telegraph, 11th February 2011

Sergeant Richard Sainsbury, who served with the South Yorkshire force for 34 years, said every officer he knew could cite examples where criminals had been allowed to go free because the Crown Prosecution Service (CPS) refused to bring charges:

'The CPS glibly dismisses evidence that a jury should see and hear. I can think of ten jobs where bad men and women should have gone to jail and who in many cases never even went to court.

'When will the likes of the justice secretary realise that prison works?'

Increase in serious offending by offenders on probation

The Guardian, 2nd August 2017

More criminals escaping with a slap on the wrist

The Daily Mail, 19th January 2021

The Chief Inspector of Probation Justine Russell said: 'More out-of-court disposals have been given in crimes reported during the pandemic. It will mean people will be getting cautions, probably with conditions attached, rather than going to court.

'This could mean serious offenders go unpunished.

'We have grave concerns that this impact will prove highly damaging to victims, witnesses and defendants.'

Note: *This statement implies that the problem of serious offenders going unpunished is new and associated with the COVID crisis. This is highly deceptive. The government's own figures show that this has been a reality for several decades.*

UK's youngest convicted terrorist can be freed, says Parole Board

The Guardian, 18th January 2021

The man, known only as RXJ, was 14 years old when he played a key role in a plot to murder police officers in Australia.

They were to be killed either with a car or by being beheaded.

RXJ is to be released after serving only five years of a life sentence. He will be subject to the following licence conditions.

Living at a specified address

Monitoring via an electronic tag

Regular appointments to check he is not relapsing

Restrictions on his movement, contacts and access to technology

Note: *The pretend nature of these restrictions is obvious. Unless a policeman lives with him 24 hours a day, it will be impossible to make sure all of them are kept. In addition, because he has been given life-long anonymity, he can go into permanent hiding, making it impossible for the community to keep an eye on him.*

The active support and help of the public in the supervision of a criminal of this kind is vital, but it has been deliberately blocked. The justice system has rated the safety of RXJ above that of the public.

'Crossbow cannibal' told he will die in prison for killing three women

The Guardian, 21st December 2010

Who is the Crossbow Killer? Stephen Griffiths' life and crimes under the spotlight

Yorkshire Live, 21st December 2010

In December 2010, criminology student Stephen Griffiths, who called himself the Crossbow Cannibal, was sentenced to a whole-life term of imprisonment.

At Leeds Crown Court, he pleaded guilty to killing three women: Susan Rushworth, 43, Shelley Armitage, 31, and Suzanne Blamires, 36.

At the time he committed these murders, he was studying for a doctorate in homicide studies at Bradford University.

A medical examination declared him to be sane and fit to plead.

Griffiths has a violent past. He battered and abused his girlfriends; in 1991, he was sentenced to two years' imprisonment for possession of an offensive weapon and causing an affray.

Aged 17, he was arrested for shoplifting and slashed the security guard's throat with a knife. He was jailed for three years but served two years, due to automatic remission.

Note: *If the reader had his or her throat cut, would he or she consider two years in jail a sufficient punishment for the attacker?*
A life sentence of imprisonment would have matched the malignity of his attack on the security guard. The three-year sentence came nowhere near punishing him for what he did. As a result of this misplaced lenience, he was left free to continue his violence.

Freed to kill again – and again: Theodore Johnson and the truth about domestic violence

The Guardian, 3rd January 2018

In 1981, Johnson killed his wife by throwing her over the balcony of their ninth-floor flat.

He was convicted of manslaughter and sentenced to three years in jail.

In 1992, he strangled his girlfriend. He was allowed to plead diminished responsibility because of 'depression'.

He was sent to a psychiatric hospital. He was released after two years with the condition he tell the authorities if he made new relationships with women.

He failed to keep this condition, and in 2016 he battered 51-year-old Angela Best to death with a claw hammer. A few days before, he had been seen by a psychiatrist who declared he was not depressed.

He was convicted of Angela Best's murder and given a life sentence with a tariff of 26 years.

Note: *Once again, remarkably lenient, not to say privileged, sentences for murderous violence allowed Johnson to kill twice after his first conviction. At that point, he could have been imprisoned for ever or for most of his life. Instead, he was given just three years' imprisonment, and with the remission of one third of his sentence, released after serving two years. Even after three killings, he has not been given a full life sentence.*

Rochdale grooming gang leader gets 22 years for child rape

'Unpleasant and hypocritical bully' Shabir Ahmed, 59, sentenced in separate trial over abusing Asian girl for ten years

The Guardian, 2nd August 2012

In May 2012, Ahmed was convicted at Liverpool Crown Court, along with eight other men, for numerous sex offences against children. He was jailed for 19 years.

In June, he was convicted separately for 30 rapes against an Asian girl whom he had been abusing for more than a decade. He was sentenced to 22 years.

Note: *Those who believe that this amounts to 41 years' imprisonment will be disappointed. The second sentence of 22 years was set to run concurrently with the first sentence of 19 years. This means he received an additional three years for 30 child rapes.*

This represents five weeks' imprisonment for each rape, an offence for which the maximum sentence is life imprisonment.

Ex-Serviceman convicted of Cat Killing

The Daily Telegraph, 31st July 2021

Hove Crown Court sentenced Steve Bouquet to five years and three months for killing nine cats and injuring seven others.

This represents four months' imprisonment for each of the 16 offences.

Note: *This is to be compared with the five-week sentence for each of Shabir Ahmed's 30 rapes against a child.*

Tougher Sentences Call

The Daily Mail, 22nd January 2016

A police constable has pleaded for tougher sentences for assaults on officers.

She had been chased by a machete-wielding drunk who avoided jail.

PC Nicholas said she had been violently attacked on three separate occasions, and each time the offender received a suspended sentence.

Note: *Is it not time that a review system was introduced that enabled judges to be held to account for the decisions they make?*

Judge praised 'brave' triple child killer, months before his murders

HM Inspectorate of Probation
Statement regarding the case of Damien Bendall
Press Release, December 2022
The Daily Telegraph, 25th December 2022

In July 2021, Damien Bendall appeared before Swindon Crown Court to be sentenced for arson. He had poured petrol over a BMW car and set it alight.

Over the previous decade, Bendall had already established himself as a dangerous criminal. His numerous previous convictions included grievous bodily harm, robbery with violence and attempted robbery.

Despite the seriousness of the arson offence and his violent past, Judge Jason Taylor KC passed a suspended 17-month prison sentence.

A probation officer's report had persuaded the judge to see Bendall as a reformed character. Errors in the probation assessment allowed the judge to conclude that the arson was 'an isolated incident' and that Bendall was 'genuinely remorseful' and had taken steps to address his problems with substance abuse.

He congratulated the offender's 'brave decision' to move away from Swindon to 'start afresh' with his partner, Terri Harris.
Before he freed Bendall, the judge said he did not think 'for a second' that he would be back in court again.

Quadruple Killer Damien Bendall Given a Whole-Life Sentence

The Derbyshire Times, 30th December 2022
MailOnline, 21st December 2022

In September 2021, three months after he had been released on a 17-month suspended prison sentence for arson, 31-year-old Damien Bendall murdered his partner, Terri Harris, 35, and her two children, Lacey Bennett, 11, and John Bennett, 13. He also murdered Lacey's 11-year-old friend Connie Gent.

He killed them with a claw hammer. His partner, Terri, was pregnant at the time of the attack. He raped 13-year-old Lacey as she lay dying.

At the time of these slayings, he was electronically tagged, in addition to being subject to the suspended sentence.

Bendall was handed five whole-life orders at Derby Crown Court on 21st December 2022, meaning he will never be released from prison

Note: *The public are now safe from Bendall; yet the door has been closed well and truly after the horse has bolted.*

The courts had the opportunity to stop Bendall in his tracks long before he committed the four murders, but failed in their duty. For a previous offence of grievous bodily harm, he was given four and a half years in prison. This means time spent in jail was little more than two years for a crime which carries a maximum sentence of life in prison. Had he been given sentences which reflected the seriousness of his previous crimes, he would not have been free to murder four people and rape one of them.

The probation officer was sacked for assessing Bendall as being of 'medium risk' to the public, instead of 'high risk'. Yet these differing categories of risk are known to be meaningless. The majority of serious further offences committed by criminals under probation supervision have been assessed as 'low risk'.

No one, including the probation service, has special skills which allow them to decide if an offender is safe to be released.

It is the senior management of the probation service who are guilty of pretending they can manage dangerous offenders in the community and protect the public.

They should have had the courage to refuse to accept this duty, laid upon them by a justice system which is indifferent to its impact on members of the public.

Is it not the case that even if the judge had the means to know for certain that Bendall would not offend again, he still should have been punished for what he did?

This case is by no means an isolated example. Hundreds (possibly thousands) of offenders have been released, assessed as 'acceptable risks' to the public, and have gone on to kill, rape and maim again.

And finally:
The following advertisement was published by the Ministry of Justice in
The Guardian, 15th November 2008

This is what the advert said:

We've changed the very heart of justice. You'll give it the new voice to match.

We're transforming the Criminal Justice System. The reforms we're implementing put the victims of crime, witnesses and members of the community at its heart – and it's time that we started to spread the good news.

Which is exactly where your professional communication skills come in.

We have opportunities across three areas of communications – Stakeholder, E-Comms and Staff Communications (including internal, regional and frontline). And whichever area you're best suited for, you'll find yourself playing a pivotal part in telling our story.

Whether you're liaising with colleagues across the Criminal Justice System, delivering messages to staff, or engaging with staff, or delivering messages to victims of crime, witnesses or the public, you'll help to make sure everyone in the country hears about the work we've already done – and our vision for the future too.
Communications Team Leaders, London £44,138–£65,975

To find out more, visit www.ocjrcommsjobs.co.uk
Closing date 10 December 2008

Joining up Justice

Ministry of Justice is an equal opportunities employer

What was the good news to be spread by the successful candidate for this post? It's not likely to have included the main trends in British criminal justice, which have dominated the public's experience of crime since 1960, and still do.

These include:

Dramatic fall in the use of imprisonment

Doubling of the homicide rate since 1964

Hundreds of killers released from a 'life' sentence to kill again

Releasing prisoners at the halfway or two-thirds point of their sentence

Significant rise in violent (and other) crime. In 1950, there were 14.3 violent offences against the person, per 100,000 of the population. There are now more than 1,400

Lower proportion of crimes recorded

Fewer criminals caught

Fewer criminals prosecuted

Increased reliance on 'rehabilitation' programmes for criminals

Persistent failure of 'rehabilitation' programmes to stop offenders from committing crime

Remanding violent and dangerous criminals on bail (and more recently without bail) rather than remanding them in prison

Continued violent criminality of offenders waiting trial or sentence in the community

Continued problem of intimidation of witnesses by offenders waiting trial

Massive increase in the legal aid bill for criminals

It is not uncommon to have muggers released

on bail eight or nine times before they face trial for their first attack.

Nothing is more contrary to the purposes of justice than the

frequent sight of robbers, and other criminals, with strings of previous convictions,

strutting across the estates of inner cities, having won their

most recent game in court – arrogant, untouchable,

fearless

and

ready for anything.

Epilogue

This book gives grounds both for optimism and pessimism. It establishes that the penalties for committing crime in Britain are often, or usually, so slight that the real question is not so much why there is so much crime but why there is so little.

The optimistic point, of course, is that most people have no desire or inclination, punishment or not, to commit crimes. And no one wants a society in which people behave well only because they fear punishment if they do not. In general, we have such a society; I am confident that readers would not steal from their neighbours even if they could be absolutely certain of getting away with it.

But we should not blind ourselves to the obvious fact that not everyone is like this, and that there are some people who are tempted to commit crimes. One of the factors most of them take into consideration in deciding whether or not to do so is what is likely to happen to them afterwards. The answer appears to be 'Not much'.

The grounds for pessimism are that despite abundant evidence of failure, the criminal justice system persists in its leniency and thereby also persists in subjecting the population to the consequences of that leniency. It will never be possible to eliminate crime altogether, but that is no excuse for not doing what is obviously possible without falling into brutality.

Theodore Dalrymple

Footnote

If the Minister of Transport continued to insist that bridges be built with plywood and plasticine in defiance of known, reliable evidence which showed that such methods resulted in injury and death for thousands of people, he or she would either be referred for psychiatric examination or face manslaughter charges.

Many might think this is a far-fetched analogy yet it fits exactly what is going on in our criminal justice system. Sixty years of evidence has shown beyond doubt that lenient sentencing practices have failed to reform criminals, and emboldened their criminality. The results for the public have been loss of life, maiming and often grievous loss an alarming scale.